YOU DON'T BELIEVE IN LOVE? HAHAHA! TRY ME!

AF428990

Dilna Mahendran

ISBN
Paperback 979-8-89475-968-5
Hardcase 979-8-89519-879-7

Contents

Dedication

The book is dedicated to Amma who was my confidante and who was my pillar of strength, to a friend who chooses to be anonymous, without whose support this book would not have seen the light of the day. This book is also dedicated to those who believed in me! My dad, my sister, my son, my teachers, my husband, who stuck with me like a rock during trying times and recognizes the writer in me and to my big big family filled with emotional and non-emotional folks! A heartfelt gratitude to my cousin Rohit Ramesh, Director, International Recruitment, York University who asked me to publish my work, Anirudh Krishnadas, my childhood friend who is kind enough to allow me to use his photographs for this book, and who makes it a point to catch up every time he comes to India. A special thanks to Ms. Shyla Mohan, former teacher and present Director of Ved Vyas Inner Space for reviewing my poems and inspiring me to write better, Mr. Pradyu Mukund M, my English teacher, who made me fall in love with the English language and who quoted seeing my work "Sylvia Plath in the making", I don't know sir, but I shall strive. A special thanks to Dr. Salil Varma (English Professor, Devagiri college) for taking out the time despite his busy schedule to review my poems. A huge gratitude to my uncle Mr. N. Asokan (Former Chief of News Bureau, Mathrubhumi) for helping me push my work, my father-in-law, Mr. N. Vijayan for encouraging me and my aunt Ms. Vidya Selvaraj for helping me connect to the right people. Thank you!

Prologue

It is a blessing and a curse to be oversensitive and this collection of poems is a testament to the beauty and burden of feeling everything deeply. These verses come from wearing my heart on my sleeve, from being unapologetically sensitive to the world around me- whether it is the tender ache of love, the gentle warmth of affection or the haunting shadow of death.

I have always felt that to live is to feel and to feel is to live with intensity. This collection captures the rawness and the richness of a life lived with an open heart.

In a world that asks us to mute our existence and our emotions, to retreat into the background to confirm to its expectations, I find myself rebelling. Through my poems I question the absurdity of such expectations and to challenge the notion that to be emotional is to be weak. As a woman and for every woman I know or have known that we are far more than the roles we play- more than daughters, mothers, sisters or wives. We are fighters and lovers, rebels and nurturers, creators and destroyers, each of us a beautiful paradox in our own right.

That being said, this book is not meant for only women, rather they are a tribute to anyone who lives or tries to live their life on their own terms and embodies that spirit.

This is my way of raising a toast to the people who refuse to be defined by a single label, who embrace their contradictions, live fully and feel deeply.

They are for those like me, see strength in sensitivity and power in vulnerability. Here's to fighters, lovers, dreamers and the rebels. Here's to those who feel and who never stop.

I hope you enjoy reading them as much as I enjoyed bringing them to creation.

About the Author

Dilna Mahendran was born in Thalasherry to Mr. Mahendran and Ms. Ajitha Mahendran. She has a loving elder sister, Sapna. She did her schooling in "Eastwood High School, Bangalore", "Our Own English High School, Dubai", "Chinmaya Vidyalaya, Kannur" and SN Vidya Mandir, Kannur. She completed her Diploma in Computer Engineering from NTTF, Bangalore.

Dilna went on to join the workforce at the age of 21 years, right after college, as a Test Engineer with Larsen and Toubro Infotech (Mumbai and Bangalore). She was promoted to Senior position. She left the organization after 4 years of service to join Ramyam Intelligence Lab, a startup in Bangalore as a Quality Analyst where she worked for a year. Marriage required her to move to Delhi where she started her freelance writing work for Digital Electronic Gadgets. Her journey then took her to Kozhikode, where she worked with Software Associates, a firm based in Kozhikode as a Digital Marketing Executive where she continued to serve for a year. She then went on to become a mother worked full-time raising her son for 6 years after which she returned to the work force with full swing as an HR and Business Development Executive for Calico Infosystems Pvt. Ltd, Hyderabad based firm in Kozhikode where she currently works.

She is also a professional voice over artiste, for a cartoon "Jhoom Tarara" with Bhooshan's Junior and also has collaborated for ad campaigns with different firms.

She is married to Mr. Thejas Vijayan ("Califab", Owner), son of Mr. N. Vijayan and Ms. Geetha Vijayan. She has a lovely 8-year-old son, master Kabir Thejas.

Ms. Dilna has always been a writer in her core. She wishes to embark on her journey in writing by taking a step in publishing her first work through this book.

1

Fairy Tale Lost in Time

My hands long to hold yours.

My heart skips a beat to listen to yours.

The void makes a second look like years fantasizing the possibility of a

wonderland filled with chatter and laughter we could have shared

The rush of waters gushing to calm a thundering storm till the star-studded night appears to

tell the story of a fairy tale lost in time.

2

Multiverse

Thinking you breathe when I breathe makes me want to smile.

The thought that as I take my brush you would be applying paste in another

verse, makes me want to move.

The thought that as I comb my hair you would be gleaming

to see my love for you in the mirror makes me want to

dance

The thought that as I prepare tea in my kitchen your blue cup I imagine

would fill up makes me want to fly like a pigeon who is seated by your

window sill cooing, to watch you take a sip of my ecstasy pump up

your tired eyes makes me feel like the melting ice.

The thought that my worn out watch would tick to the last second to open

the glass doors of time and spaces between us makes me get lost in my

thoughts of the multiverse.

3

Walking Home with Her

Did time travel with my younger sister.

She and I foraged for fruits of laughter and fun we once shared

In the wild lanes covered by golden and green leaves from grand trees,

in a kitchen that smelled of burning wood and soot, of ripe jackfruits

and mangoes,

the juice of which trickled from the sides of our mouth,

our tongues trying to divert it back to where it belonged.

She and I fixed the puzzle. She fixed my missing

pieces and I hers, of an ancestral home Rich with

the Simplicities of "LOVE" and "CARE"

In which every window was wide open

to a world full of possibilities.

4

Forgiveness

Like a shriveled leaf
hanging by a miracle
I spin and spin to the breeze, a breeze that
whispers words of love and that whispers words
of a jealous lover of ours

But despite the odds my want to pour in love to your heart
continues I know not once you will look back
For the lanes we once tread you are trying to erase, the done
you are trying to undo the bricks of ego, pride and
misunderstanding have been laid... The green leaves may
dance ever so gracefully around you and this shriveled leaf
would probably go unnoticed

My flaws are bright as the morning sunlight today the rays of
which just want to pierce your soul for forgiveness for having
gone blind to the untainted side of yours.

5

Forbidden Territory

My age shreds me.
It shreds and sheds
Cutting me piece by piece like a slice of cake!

One day as my body withers away and the brown blends with the dirt and the mud,
insects and birds will eat my carcass leaving behind my bones

Stories, poems and gossips would feed the hungry vultures
Whose minds flash and dim, flash and dim and contradict
themselves

I don't wish to be in love or loved
I wish to be by a pianist, listening to the keys shift the mood in me
I would love to decipher the soul in silence as I bring order to the chaos around me,
I wish to feed my soul with adventures of a solitary bliss
where black letters in white spaces take me to a secret garden and unseen landscapes
inorder to give me a rush
To dance in the "forbidden territory".

6

Trance

When I talk to you, I run a full circle
You make me tread a path I am very familiar with
so familiar that I can run blindly and tell the season
before it arrives

Every conversation starts with an inflation of the ego
making me feel how lucky I am,
My eyeballs once round turn to a uniform spiral
which leads to a map of your favorite places to tread
Paris, India and Hiroshima in the end.

Whatever remains becomes my purpose
How? What? Why?

For our friction with life I wish I had a panacea but I realized over the period of time
That we are numb, blind, deaf and mute to this very existence

We are nothing but poker-faced zombies who
smother ourselves with optimism To tread the
circle all over again! ☺

7

Life or Death

You cast a spell

I learn to speak

You cast a spell

I learn to walk

You cast a spell

I learn to run

You cast a spell

I learn and learn

To love, to hate, to care, to be insensitive, to like, to dislike, to

laugh, to cry, to weave my dreams into reality…

We dance

You smile and gently hold my hand…

Slyly, you rob away every penny I earned… "Your new lover

is very popular, some go slow, some go fast" (I whisper in

your ears and doubt…)

Knock! Knock!

(I open…)

(I look back at you aghast)

How dare you invite your muse?

(I stare into the blank)

Not knowing who will eat me first

You or your new muse, slow or fast…

8

Betrayal

She poured and poured

She shouted, she screamed, she cut herself to

pieces and put the other before her to build a castle.

Her castle now surrounded by trained soldiers

Who are her lifeline?

Who love her?

but restrain her from painting, the very art she knew.

she befriended a canvas despite the odds, surrounded herself

and made her life the empathetic canvas…

She talks to the canvas and tries to paint designs the canvas has never seen.

The canvas whispers and reassures how her every stroke would be unique and special.

The canvas she tried to water and paint with colours not seen by the earthlings.

She took her brush and made strokes so gentle and drew lifelike images never before seen.

She didn't care about the hours spent to paint the canvas, the ways she tricked the

soldiers to paint her life like strokes, the times she dipped her brush in unique hues,

the number of strokes she made thinking the canvas would soak the unfamiliar shades.

The colours wiped her sweat with traces of paint on her forehead and cheeks

The paint faded away by night leaving her blank and in disbelief!

The canvas dried and showed traces of the usual prints she had seen painted by the commoners

making her stroke look ordinary and uninspiring..

She erased and tried again but the canvas showed her that the print is not exquisite.

Now the canvas wants to devour her alive, her blood, her sweat, her everything.

She now longs to leave the castle and the canvas and be by the plants and the trees

who effortlessly understand her and who make her feel special and magical, the

fluttering of the butterflies, the carols of the birds who accept her without her

speaking a single word and without a single stroke of her brush.

9

Mystic Holi

One drop fell

Another , another and another

The sound became stronger

and louder.

It played a symphony of a mellifluous rainfall

She giggled, her friend giggled

The sceptical giggled, the stressed giggled

The giggles turned to laughter and it reverberated

till it hit the drums so loud, so loud… that people started to bounce up and down the trampoline

The mixed colours made one forget the self and it brought back the beats of a forest, fire and a

rhythm between man and man,

man and woman, woman and woman, old and young, and for

once they forgot the clans or the tribes they belonged to each

colour blending so harmoniously.

The ray passed from one soul to another and to another like the light

through the prism

"A rainbow amidst the scatter.."

10

Constant

Constant is
What to do?
What not to do?
The pressure of the eyes watching you
exhale and inhale
judging why you lost flesh,
why you gained, why your hair fell to
lighten the pressure you are dealing
with, by the day.

The arena is doped with people who think
they know, who act like gods and who stoop
their backs when needed who justify every
action and rebuke another's

My straight lines are no longer straight
They are twisted as my soul feeds curves
curves that bend and bend to a hopeless dead end or a hopeful tomorrow

Hope is fed to balance the pots on my head as I
walk on a rope without a safety net below me.

I'd rather tread on a path I colour and craft
one that I weave out of my imagination

Than fall, fall, and fall from a rope
designed by the clueless.

I'd rather tread on a path I colour and craft

11

Reality Bites

Glad that you exist!

Glad that you painted the leaves green

Left splashes of colours with flowers on the bed

Glad you made the birds sing

Coz when the mind wanders

You grab me by your arms, take me from my juxtaposed frames of yester

and morrow and erect me into the real

I touch you for real this time accepting this very fact and oh!

What do I feel?

The dust left by yesterday?

I will wipe the dust, will remove the cobwebs

But still with a smile you will remind me that

we exist between yesterday and today

I don't wish to wipe you anymore

No, No, No

Coz I know the rains will do that

I don't wish to tame you anymore

No, No, No

Because you existed before I came and will exist after I leave

I just want to be seated with you

unperturbed by what goes and what comes

I want to hear you sing without dolby sounds

that blends oh so beautifully

with my imaginary world that once existed…hahaha..but now no more.

feeling as light as the breeze with empty spaces around me.

The wind is blowing and I am feeling light, oh so light…whoosh!!! to be

blown away by the very dust left by the same like my mother read or

can it be a different breeze???

12

A Mother Daughter from Different Realms

She slid down the rainbow to meet the unicorns who carry messages
from her mother from the far away land the messages will unravel
each day-a unicorn will come with sunlight, a unicorn will come with
rain, a unicorn will come with other surprises to brighten up her
everyday
The beautiful laughter of her mother will tickle her and make her laugh

She will become the dream through the secret messages her mother gift wrapped

"Each and every day."

13

My Magical Pouch

I have a pouch
A magical little pouch with prints of fossils of lightning

It carries memories of a seed that remained from a love bite

The heartbeat of the seed anxious and confused hundred and sixty by
the minute due to the unsteady tides and storms her tumultuous ship
underwent

The pouch became huge and heavy and left no room for empty spaces until the green clad
midwives emptied the pouch to find a beautiful boy from the seed he secretly left behind In her
pouch

Running,   Stretching,   Bending   and
Twisting

The pouch is still not empty as it carries memories of a
journey of three in the body of one.

14

Freedom to Love

"She is mine"

"He is mine"

"I will love her"

"I will love him"

"I will not eat till he comes home"

"I am doomed if she dies"

"I am doomed if he dies"

"She is a melodrama"

"He is a prick"

"She is a slut"

"I wasted time with him/ her"

Nobody is no one's

Smile, laugh when you can

With whoever you are with

And let go…

You are free…

15

Earth is Melting

Are you burning?

Are you melting like a candle?

What happened to the god you were trying to be?

The act of knowing it all

The act of studying me intricately

Atom, molecule, bacteria, amoeba

History, geography, mathematics

You dissected me, you conducted meetings, and ruled over me.

What good?

Today I see smoke everywhere

From chimneys to factories

I see froth of sulphur in the rivers I gave you pure

I see mountains of garbage

That you refuse to clean up

I see slums and huge buildings

In a forest where you were free

I see psychological distress in the rules

You set for yourself Trying to

appease one another.

What to do?

Hahaha

You are the god now…you decide.

16

Break the Wall

I move left, I read a quote and I lay a brick

there

I move right, I hear a journey

I lay a brick there

Finally I decide to do something worthwhile

And I look around

And there are bricks everywhere lol

Making me immobile

In a world full of opportunities

A world not built of bricks

But blue skies, green grass, fresh water and sweet berries

Whose very fate changed because of the greed of man.

17

First Move

Will he?

Will I?

Will we?

Will my pen write a poem

To trace the emptiness, I feel today?

Will I feel the raindrop on my chapped lips again?

Will I dance, bare feet on the wet earth again?

Will I ever see a notification that makes my heart beat thousands of drums by the minute?

My aged hands tread a thousand miles to gently stroke your hair

I am seated before you

Nonchalantly listening to your ailing heart…

Your delirious thoughts in soaring temperature will abate, my dear

And my love will keep you warm in your freezing days.

18

Sip of Love

One cup to another

You pour your focus, care and love

Long curve and short

Long curve and short

Making the steam infused with tea and milk

Fill up my soul

Before the first sip

Cooling down from piping hot

To warm cozy comfort for my gentle lips

The frothy bubbles tightly pack the flavour

As you hand over the glass

I once again cling on to the needles of time

To a memory of a kitchen with mother and aunts

Smiling and giggling

Interrupted by the gentle alarm

Of my name being called out and a smile to say

PASS ON THE LOVE

19

Decaying Love

Don't know how to express my love to you
Am I in love?
I am deaf when you call me and you deaf when I call you
Are we in love?

If you are sick I am insensitive
Am I in love?
If you need water I ask you to
Go and take it
Am I in love?

If you ask me for a tissue twice
My blood boils
Am I in love?

You need love and care
Like a mom
Am I a lover or a mom?
Am I in love?

20

Scream

"Buy, consume!"

Bakeries, Restaurants, Malls, Pharmacies, Hospitals More

Bakeries, Restaurants, Malls, Pharmacies and Hospitals

ATMs!

"Withdraw and consume!"

"Buy 1 get 2 free"

"Upto 50% off"

"Sale! Mega Sale!"

"Withdraw and consume!"

Roads connecting each other

Screaming out from each side

"Buy, Consume!"

Making every curve look

Uninteresting, straight and standard

If the roads connected each other without these boards

How would life be?

If there were only fresh produce, art and music of the locals,

And those who want to join the clan

Blend, sing and dance

How would life be?

If there were no crooked and cunning If

honesty, trust, love and good friendship grew

How would life be?

If only money was taken out of the equation of life

How would life be?

21

Ant to Human - God is Relative

I carry a dust particle

Suddenly a shower

The dust turned to a sandstone

Unflustered I carried it

Eyes were blinded by the gigantic drops that nearly drowned me

My brothers and sisters signalled to me that I need to hurry

To build the anthill we had in our plan

So despite the odds I carried it.

As I looked to see around

I saw two eyes staring, reflection showed a rufous treepie

Hop from a wet leaf above me to another

after the spell of rain

Causing the downpour I was experiencing

The eyes unaware of the "One" hopping

From one cloud to another

22

Erotic Love

Come Walk!

Walk with me on this lonely road

Step with me into the endless layers, shapes of green, triangles, rounded curves and clovers

Featherlike hands Wanting

to touch thy curves

Come Lie!

Come Lie down with me, naked.

Don't carry no luggage

We don't need the baggages of our timeline

Come Feel!

Come Feel with me the quiet shower

When the magic spell stops…

Come Gaze!

Come Gaze with me into the crystals

Left behind by the droplets making

the present more like a dream

Don't Hope!

Don't hope to seek the future in them

Just gaze..

Come Stare!

Come Stare with me

My ceiling now the endless skies

Where clouds of cotton

Grey and white dance in ethereal fashion

Come Make Love!

Come make love with me to the orchestra set by the birds near and

far, a gentle breeze to caress

Our souls

Come make love with me like snakes intertwined to meet the climax of another universe

Come Laugh!

Come laugh with me

As thy blesses us with a magic spell everyday

Finally Rejoice and Smile!

Rejoice and smile with me to be part of

God's Wild, Eccentric and GRAND PLAN!

• • •

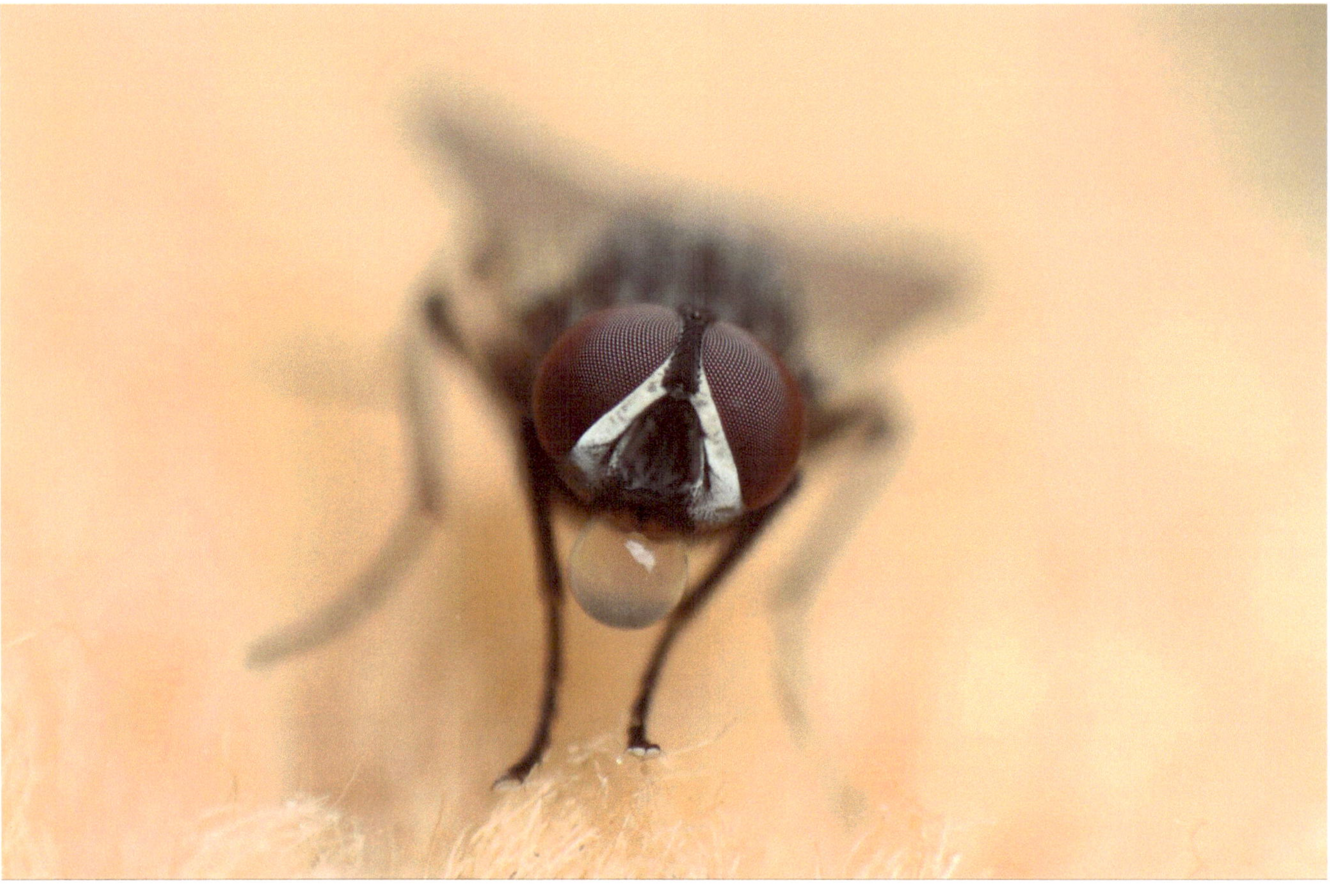

23

Houseflies

The tongues came out to taste the sea of my turbulence with the everyday act

Hands rubbed in delight to touch me

My eyes, lips, curves and that which was exposed

The eyeballs bulge out in fascination

Hahaha!

Forgetting the alphonsos which are in season now.

The hands and the tongue together

played a melody with my crazy mind as they tickled and licked every inch

To see if I was ripe enough in order to signal to the predators

Who glide, soar and circle me everyday

To watch the transition of my skin

From supple to wrinkled

The odour from the perfumed to the nonenal

My third eye opened

I shooed the buggers

And roared

JUST NOT YET!

-

24

Measure

Your height is between the ground below your feet and the endless expanse of sky above you.

Your length is your potential to spread a smile around you..

Your width depending on what you choose for yourself

And your volume, my love, is the capacity to hold light inside you after the sun has set.

25

Doubt

Is my love a full stop or a comma?

Am I enough or not?

Eyebrows furrow

I withdraw

The fog of doubt spreads and thickens

Blinding the vision of a table

That was once occupied by

The crude and the naked

Both seated in their attempt

To play their cards

To show to each other

A full house of hearts

26

Live in Real

Don't life in the fictitious
Or else you'd be robbed
Of the pleasures of the real

The smell of the royal jasmine, the grit of the mud under your feet,
The odour of the soap to the sweat
That reminds you of the onions you cut for dinner last night

Sink into the abyss the earth offers you
For below the untamed wild lies the fossil
That is calm and resting
For another to discover

Let not fear conquer your footsteps
That are intended to cause a flame
That will ignite you from within
To keep you away from your darkest hour!

27

Tonight's Lover

I cuddle up to you
To smell the memory of
Yesterday's passion
My lips pressed against yours
My creeper like leg wraps around you
Hoping to not let go of you
Not even in the deepest of sleep

You give me a sense of permanence in a rickety rackety world
You choose to not react or respond to my blows
You accept the weight of my thighs
And give comfort to every cell of mine making me feel
as light as the cotton stuffed inside you
After a day's sweat and blood.

28

Paradise

Home-> School-> College->Friend's/ Lover's/ Relative's home

Again Home

Home-> Restaurant/ Mall/ Park/Gym->Home

Again Home

Home-> Hostel->Home

Again Home

Hostel-> Pub-> Hostel-> Home

Again Home

Home-> Office->Home

Again Home

Home-> Vacation->Home

Again Home

Home-> Restaurant/ Mall/ Park/Gym->Home Home->

Ambulance-> Hospital->?

WELCOME! One

Paradise to another

GOD'S HOME!

29

Hope

When the fungus eats the inside
Tries to infect you
With thoughts that gnaw you

A strand of light falls on a green leaf
That shares a story
Making you forget about the itch of death
Lurking around the corner

The green leaf talks of a story
To live young when you are young
And laugh your ass off when you are old

Yourself you seen another time
Through the lens of those
Who immerse their time in you
Time is money they say And you
feel valuable once again

The cure is found!
The fungus is gone!
There is hope once again! The
leaf once eaten by the fungus
Is GREEN again!

30

Wake Me Up Gently

Isn't it beautiful to simply exist?
Like leaves swaying to the breeze
No music but rustling of these leaves
No humans to intervene

Colours of flowers to lift your sleepy eyes
Perfumes of which are so gentle
You forget your problems

Green and Brown equally beautiful
One is the real and one in the unreal.

31

Build Again

I don't wish to write on the dots

Laid by you

I will place the dots

Where my calling takes me

One dot far and another near

The writing maybe curved or zig-zag

You may not even understand my writing

And I don't wish for you to understand

EYES, EVIL EYES, POSITIVE, NEGATIVE rule the day..

If you are positive you are in..

Negative, you are doomed.

Order! Order! Order!

Put everything in order

Manners! Etiquette! Behave! Hahaha!

Bring order! Be Systematic! Be Disciplined!

Till the very order identifies an ant

Gnawing the Brain

And Whoops!

HUSHA BUSHA!

We all fall down…hahaha!

GET UP! RISE UP ! BUILD AGAIN!

BECAUSE CHILD, YOUR CALLING AWAITS YOU!

32

Evolution

My body keeps evolving with time and my journey keeps

changing with time

Today's me can be a different me tomorrow

If the branch of my memory mercilessly falls to change the course of my flow

I shall accept it and flow through unknown terrains

My water I choose for it to be clear, so with my conscience as my expressions were

pure

I judge no one as our rendezvous happened in maybe ten frames out of millions

like a speck in the universe and a journey closely moving to a brighter tomorrow.

33

Ordinary

It is ok to be ordinary brown, black or grey and

blend in instead of choosing to be different

It is nice to be a building block that is part of a great plan sometimes

The Mr. and Ms. Nobody when the idea by itself is magnificent the

very idea taking the spotlight and me being behind the scenes.

It is good to be mum and let the plan flow through you.

It is wonderful to soil your hands and step into a muddy puddle

to plant a space for a better tomorrow.

34

Single or Committed?

From "Single" to "Committed" to "Single"

Why do you pose?

Are you telling me to understand your cryptic clues?

I do not wish to read these clues

I am at peace…

Your everyday conversations are now a movie like memory to me

You stage a show with me as the lead

The heroine now a villain

I'd never thought I'd step into these shoes

Was your love for real?

mocking, criticizing, playing with our everyday life

we criticize rather than empathize we draw clear

distinction between good and bad and we end up

being in each other's shoes

The good becomes the bad and the bad becomes the good.

You change my beliefs and I change yours so evidently we need not cling on to them

as they get eroded to build other escapes or escapades far away from the real

world.

35

You Will Not Drown, I Promise!

I don't wish to tell you my current location

I don't wish to share with you the last time I missed you

I don't wish to tell you what is on my mind right now I don't

want to because you consider all this futile malleable enough

to twist and bend it according to your needs

I wish to be silent and observe the direction this wave will take

me from Satan's burn to Buddha's enlightenment

my journey will be solo

and my words to you will be shallow and gift wrapped with emojis of the

" funny- faced"," the smiling" and " the happy."

Hahaha!

Shallow enough so that you don't drown in these waters

36

Share

"How are you?"

"I am fine!"

"How was your day?"

"It was ok"

Twelve hours is a mixed bag

Find Fun, Insightful talks, Dramedy

Don't just tap tap tap

Tap the real

Look up to see…

It aches to see how you don't find god in these twenty four hours

How the fluttering of a butterfly doesn't bring you joy

How the colors of flowers don't cause a smile on you boy

How you can't remember the laughter of a loved one or a stranger during the

day due to a tickle one stirred up in a conversation with what he/she had to say

It aches to see how you can't share the depths of a day and just cover it up like a

coffin with a message that says "It was ok" rather than the norm "RIP"

Next time..do better , "will you?"

37

From Love to Loveless

I rest my success and failure on you

like resting my head on a pillow

You are lifeless, your permanence gives me a sense of satisfaction

I paint my idol ugly,

I own an evil eye to burn those jealous eyes

I rely on lemons, salt and chillies to ward away the evil when in my

mind I am insecure and feel a sense of impermanence of the

riches I feel I don't deserve Why?

because I was raised to serve not to own

I was raised a second class citizen in my very own

home

I tie threads and put ashes on my forehead

to feel safe

Safe from what?

Rape? Death?

News of which runs loud and is celebrated by papers

to silence the voices of those like me.

For once listen to the other side and fix the pieces of a loveless heart

We come, we go

Are we special ?

No

Like plants, ants or any other creature

We are aliens who landed on earth to enjoy

To enjoy what?

The everyday act of being alive!

38

Three Wise Monkeys

I wish I was an idol carved to be still and smiling unaffected by the

circus outside or the prayers from the persons contradicting each

other on the inside, each being a hero in their own life

Adorned with jewellery and sarees that speak of tradition,

accepting every word because clearly

I can't say a thing!

You chant versus you hope I hear everyday

meaning of which clearly you don't understand

nor can I hear!

You make me look like a fresh bloom, a mother who can balance all walks of

life well kempt, with eyes that say I understand you

When clearly I don't feel a thing!

Adorned with fresh flowers, incense sticks , sandalwood paste, betel leaves and areca nut when

clearly I can't smell a thing!

Light from diyas to shed away darkness

when clearly I can't see a thing!

Your belief in me is so strong and

what you believe I become!

39

Lose Yourself

Tick tock tick tock
I don't want to listen to this clock
I would love for it to
silence and not run in a race
I would love to continue to write, sing, dance and paint
till my heart fills up and satiates

I don't want to think about the nutrients I had or cups of water I had
whether it met the dietician's say or the influencer's play

I want to immerse myself till I am exhausted and there is no
difference between the art, artist and me.